Welcome

Congratulations
United States citi
this momentous c ....und that this
is an exciting time for you and your family and we
are confident that Citizenship Basics© will prepare
you for that big day. As you know, U.S. citizenship
comes with many rights and privileges along with
important responsibilities and this study guide will
help you become familiar with everything you need
to know.

You can use this book to learn about U.S.
government, civics, and history. The readings are
designed to help you understand the questions you
may be asked on the day of your interview. The
vocabulary is in bold to help you recognize key
words that may be a part of both the reading and
writing portions of the exam. The ESL lessons are
designed to prepare you for the questions that may
come up from the N-400. Practice with a partner or
by yourself.

In this updated version, all names and dates are
current as of 2014 and interview questions reflect
the new N-400 application. However, due to
elections and unforeseen changes in the political
system, some information may change. This book
includes links to valuable websites so that you can
get the most current information.

We want to wish you all the best as you embark on
your journey to United States citizenship.

Sincerely,
Darin French

About the Authors

Darin French

Darin has taught U.S. History, Government, Basic Language Arts, ESL and ESL/Citizenship for the Los Angeles Unified School District since 2007. He has also served as a CBET coordinator, ESL teacher advisor, and participated on several textbook selection committees and WASC accreditation teams. He received his BA in History and Political Science from the University of California at Los Angeles.

Robert Proctor

Robert received his degree from the University of California at Santa Barbara and has been teaching children and adults for over 20 years. He has been with LAUSD since 1996 as an ESL instructor, reading instructor, and teacher advisor. He has worked on numerous textbook review committees as well as several WASC accreditation teams. Robert has co-authored several educational products, including Citizenship Basics.

Table of Contents

For permission to use material from this text or product, submit all requests to
darin@sceduserv.com

ISBN - 978-0-615-95815-6

Southern California Educational Services, LLC
4555 E. 3rd St #3B
Los Angeles, CA 90022

Also Available from This Seller:
English Basics: Your Guide to Prepositions

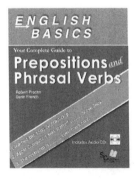

ISBN - 978-0-692-30509-6

Available at:
www.sceduserv.com

or

www.amazon.com

Citizenship Basics is not affiliated with USCIS or the U.S. Government. Citizenship Basics is only meant to be a study tool for students preparing for their U.S. naturalization interviews.

CHAPTER I

U.S. Government

★ The Constitution
★ The President
★ Congress
★ The Supreme Court
★ ESL Lesson - Present Tense

The Constitution

The Constitution was drafted in **1787** and begins with the words **"We the people."** The Constitution is **the supreme law of the land** and **sets up the government** of the United States. It gives each branch specific powers. However, a system of **checks and balances prevents one branch from becoming too powerful** over the others.

The Constitution can be **changed,** or **amended,** because the original writers understood that as the country and society changed, the Constitution needed to change with it. The first ten amendments to the Constitution are called **the Bill of Rights** and guarantee certain rights to all people living in the United States. The 1st Amendment guarantees the freedom of **speech, religion, assembly, and press.** There are currently **27 amendments** to the Constitution.

Fun Fact!

Did you know that the Constitution was actually the second attempt to form a new government? The first document, called the Articles of Confederation, was formally ratified in 1781 but later abandoned because the nationalists believed it gave too much power to the states and created a weak central government.

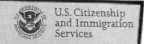 U.S. Citizenship
and Immigration
Services

Civics (History and Government) Questions for the Naturalization Test

1. What is the supreme law of the land?

2. What does the Constitution do?

3. The idea of self-government is in the first three words of the Constitution. What are these words?

4. What is an amendment?

5. What do we call the first ten amendments to the Constitution?

6. What is one right or freedom from the First Amendment?

7. How many amendments does the Constitution have?

The President

The President is in charge of the **Executive Branch** of the United States government and is elected every **four years** in **November.** The president's responsibilities include the power to **sign bills into law, veto bills,** and **serve as the commander in chief of the military.**

If the president can no longer serve, the **vice president** becomes president. Because the Executive Branch must make decisions on a variety of subjects, a cabinet is appointed to **advise the president** on specific areas such as defense, education, and commerce to name a few.

The first president of the United States was **George Washington**, who was elected in 1788 after leading the Continental Army to victory in the Revolutionary War. **Barack Obama** is the current and 44th president of the United States.

Congress

The Legislative Branch, or **Congress**, is divided into two houses: **the Senate and House of Representatives**. Both senators and representatives are chosen through direct elections. There are a total of 535 voting members in Congress: **435** members in the House of Representatives and **100** members in the Senate. Members of the House of Representatives serve **two-year terms**. The number of representatives a state has **depends on the state's population**, with each state in the union having at least one representative in the House of Representatives. Regardless of population, **each of the 50 states has two senators**; each senator serves a **six-year** term and represents **all people of the state**. The **Legislative Branch** is responsible for **making federal laws**.

Can you name your U.S. representative?

For more information on how a bill becomes law, see page 25.

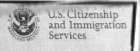
1. Who makes federal laws?

2. What are the <u>two</u> parts of the U.S. Congress?

3. How many U.S. Senators are there?

4. We elect a U.S. Senator for how many years?

5. Who is <u>one</u> of your state's U.S. Senators now?

6. The House of Representatives has how many voting members?

7. We elect a U.S. Representative for how many years?

8. Name your U.S. Representative.

9. Who does a U.S. Senator represent?

10. Why do some states have more Representatives than other states?

Fun Fact!

California has the most representatives with a total of 53.

Find your U.S. Representative by going to: http://citizenshipbasics.com/find-your-u-s-representative

The Supreme Court

The highest court in the United States is the **Supreme Court.** The Supreme Court, part of the **Judicial Branch,** decides if a law goes against the Constitution. The **nine** members, or justices, of the Supreme Court are appointed by the President and confirmed by the senate. Once confirmed, a justice serves for life. The founders believed that this would ensure that justices would not be influenced by political pressure or public passions. The current Chief Justice of the United States now is **John G. Roberts, Jr**, appointed by President George W. Bush.

Fun Fact!

Did you know that at times there have only been six justices?

For more information on the Judicial Branch, visit www.whitehouse.gov/ our-government/ judicial-branch

1. What does the judicial branch do?

2. What is the highest court in the United States?

3. How many justices are on the Supreme Court?

4. Who is the Chief Justice of the United States now?

Super Stat

■ Longest Serving Supreme Court Justices

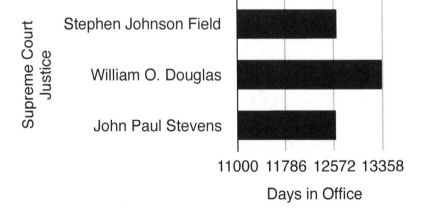

The Simple Present Tense

Use the Simple Present Tense when talking about events that happen now and are repeated or usual. Like all verb tenses it can be expressed in the negative.

> ex) I live in Los Angeles.

In this example you live in the city of Los Angeles right now.

> ex) I don't live in Las Vegas.

In this example you do not live in Las Vegas.

The Simple Present of the verb "to be"

Subject	to be	Negative
I	am	I am not
You	are	You're not You aren't
He, She, It	is	He's not, she's not, it's not He isn't, she isn't, it isn't
We	are	We're not We aren't
They	are	They're not They aren't

N-400 Application for Naturalization

Use black ink.

Here are some examples of the *Simple Present Tense* taken from the N-400 application.

1. What is your marital status?
2. Is your spouse a U.S. citizen?
3. Do you owe any Federal, State, or local taxes that are overdue?
4. Are you a member of the communist party?

Possible Answers to the above Simple Present Questions.

1. I am single.
2. Yes, she is.
3. No, I don't. (*negative*)
4. No, I'm not. (*negative*)

Your Everyday Activities

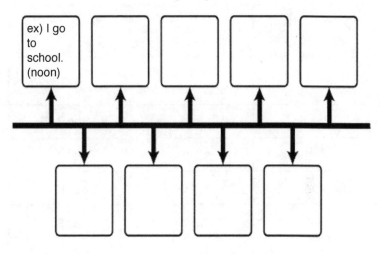

ex) I go to school. (noon)

1. **Put nine daily activities on the TIMELINE above. Then talk about them in the simple present tense with a partner.**
ex) *I go to school at noon.*
or
I work from 9:00 a.m to 5:00 pm.

or ask a question

Do you eat lunch at 2:00 p.m.?

No, I don't. I eat lunch at 12:30 p.m.

Verbs

BASE FORM	I, You, We, They	He, She, It
be	I am, (You, We, They) are	is
live	live	live<u>s</u>
study	study	studies
work	work	works
have	have	has
drive	drive	drives
go	go	goes
take	take	takes
give	give	gives

2. Write 3 sentences about your life using the simple present.

ex) I work Monday through Friday.

1._____

2._____

3._____

3. Complete each sentence in simple present tense using the verb in parentheses. ( )

1. I _____ everyday at 9 o'clock.
     (work)

2. Joe _____ in New York City.
     (live)

3. We don't _____ in Las Vegas
       (live)

4. How many children do you _____?
          (have)

5. Do you _____ a car?
     (drive)

6. My brother and sister don't _____ Japanese.
       (study)

7. Does your family ever _____ to Disneyland?
       (go)

8. She _____ care of our children.
     (take)

4. Practice the conversation with a partner.

A: Good afternoon. How are you?

B: I'm fine. And you?

A: Fine, thanks. Do you have your application?

B: Yes, I do. Here is my application.

A: And is your application completely filled out?

B: Yes, it is. It's complete.

A: Are you married or single?

B: I'm married.

A: Does your spouse work?

B: No, he/she doesn't.

A: Ok. That's all. Thank you for your time.

Questions and Responses Using Simple Present

5. Work with a partner to ask and answer the following questions.

Q: Do you ever go to Disneyland?

A: Yes, I do. / No, I don't.

Q: Do you like Sushi?

A: Yes, I do. / No, I don't.

Q: Does your son go to college?

A: Yes, he does. / No, he doesn't.

Q: Are you married?

A: Yes, I am. / No, I'm not.

Q: Is your daughter in school?

A: Yes, she is. / No, she isn't.

CHAPTER II

U.S. Civics

★ Right to Vote
★ From a Bill to a Law
★ The Electoral College
★ ESL Lesson - Past Tense

The Right to Vote

The **right to vote** is considered one of the most important rights citizens of the United States possess. It is an opportunity for every citizen over the age of **eighteen** to participate in the political process. However, it has taken many decades to guarantee this right to all eligible Americans.

The **15th Amendment** guaranteed the right to vote regardless of race, color, or previous condition of servitude. This allowed freed black men to exercise the right to vote but not women. **The 19th Amendment** gave women the right to vote by saying that this right cannot be denied based on sex. Under the **24th Amendment,** a poll tax cannot be required to vote. **The 26th Amendment** lowered the voting age from 21 to 18.

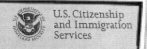

U.S. Citizenship
and Immigration
Services

Civics (History and Government) Questions for the Naturalization Test

1. There are four amendments to the Constitution about who can vote. Describe <u>one</u> of them.

2. What is <u>one</u> responsibility that is only for United States citizens?

3. Name <u>one</u> right only for United States citizens.

4. How old do citizens have to be to vote for President?

5. What are <u>two</u> ways that Americans can participate in their democracy?

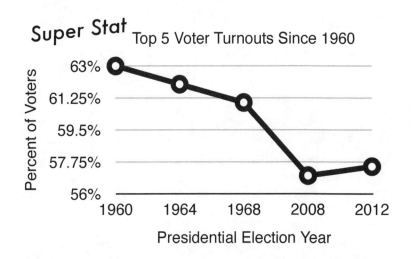

Super Stat Top 5 Voter Turnouts Since 1960

Percent of Voters: 63%, 61.25%, 59.5%, 57.75%, 56%

Presidential Election Year: 1960, 1964, 1968, 2008, 2012

The Electoral College

Many people believe that the election of the President is decided by popular vote. However, presidential elections are determined by the electoral college.

The electoral college was established by the founding fathers as a compromise between the election of the President by a vote in Congress and the election of the President by a popular vote of qualified citizens. Each state is given a certain number of electors and after the votes are counted, the Presidential candidate who wins the popular vote in that state receives all of that states' electoral votes.

A Presidential candidate must get 270 electoral votes out of 538. To learn more about the electoral college visit :

www.archives.gov/federal-register/electoral-college/about.html

From a Bill to a Law

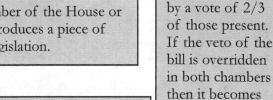

1. A member of the House or Senate introduces a piece of legislation.

2. The bill is referred to the appropriate committee by the Speaker of the House or the presiding officer of the Senate.

8. Congress can override the veto by a vote of 2/3 of those present. If the veto of the bill is overridden in both chambers then it becomes law.

3. The bill is debated on in the House and Senate.

7. If the President vetoes the bill, it is sent back to Congress with a note listing his or her objections.

4. The bill is voted on and if the House and Senate pass the bill, it is sent to the President.

6. The bill becomes law if signed by the President or if not signed within 10 days and Congress is in session.

5. The President reviews the bill.

The Simple Past Tense

Use the Simple Past Tense when talking about events that happened in the past and ended in the past. Like all verb tenses it can be expressed in the negative.

ex) I lived in New York for two years.

In this example you lived in the city of New York for two years, but not anymore.

ex) I didn't live in Las Vegas.

In this example you did not live in Las Vegas.

The Simple Past of the verb "to be"

Subject	to be	Negative
I	was	I wasn't
You	were	You weren't
He, She, It	was	He wasn't, She wasn't, It wasn't
We	were	We weren't
They	were	They weren't

N-400 Application for Naturalization

Use black ink.

Here are some examples of the *Simple Past Tense* taken from the N-400 application.

---

1. How many total days <u>did</u> you spend outside of the United States?
2. <u>Did</u> the trip last six months or more?
3. When <u>did</u> your spouse become a citizen?
4. What schools <u>did</u> you attend?
5. I <u>prepared</u> this application.

Possible Answers to the above Simple Present Questions.

1. I <u>spent</u> thirty days outside of the U.S.
2. No, it <u>didn't</u>.
3. She (he) <u>became</u> a citizen in 1997.
4. I <u>attended</u> UCLA.
5. Yes, I <u>did</u>. I <u>prepared</u> this application.

Your Important Life EventVerbs

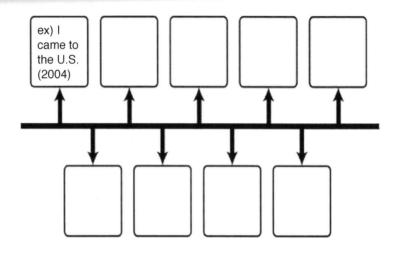

1. **Put nine important life events on the TIMELINE above. Then talk about them in the simple past tense with a partner.**
   ex) *I came to the U.S. in 2004.*
   or
   I moved to Texas last year.

   or ask a question

   Did you move to Florida in 2010?

   No, I didn't. I moved to Texas last year.

Verbs

BASE FORM	SIMPLE PAST
come	came
live	lived
study	studied
work	worked
have	had
drive	drove
go	went
take	took
give	gavew

2. Write 3 sentences about your life using the simple past.

ex) I worked yesterday.

1._____

2._____

3._____

3. Complete each sentence in simple past tense using the verb in parentheses. ( )

1. I _____ everyday last week.
   (work)

2. Joe _____ in New York City for a year.
   (live)

3. We didn't _____ in Las Vegas
   (live)

4. How many pets did you _____?
   (have)

5. You _____ a car to school today.
   (drive)

6. My brother and sister didn't _____ Japanese.
   (study)

7. Did your family ever _____ to Disneyland?
   (go)

8. She _____ care of our children.
   (take)

4. Practice the conversation with a partner.

A: Good afternoon. How was your drive here?

B: It was fine. Thanks.

A: Ok. Did you finish your application?

B: Yes, I did. Here it is.

A: And did you have any problems filling it out?

B: No, I didn't. It wasn't very difficult.

A: Ok. Good. Were you ever married before?

B: Yes, I was, but I was divorced in 2002.

A: Did your ex-spouse get remarried?

B: No, he (she) didn't.

A: Ok. That's all for now. I appreciate your time.

Contraction Alert!

Negative "to be" in the Simple Past
Subject Pronoun + was/were + not
I wasn't, You weren't, We weren't,
They weren't, He wasn't, She wasn't, It wasn't
I wasn't ready.
Negatives with did
did + not
didn't
No, she didn't.

Questions and Responses Using Simple Past

5. Work with a partner to ask and answer the following questions.

Q: Did you go to Disneyland yesterday?

A: Yes, I did. / No, I didn't.

Q: Were you late for work today?

A: Yes, I was. / No, I wasn't.

Q: Did your son go to college?

A: Yes, he did. / No, he didn't.

Q: Was your family from Canada?

A: Yes, they were. / No, they weren't.

CHAPTER III

U.S. History

★ Early Colonists
★ Founding Fathers
★ Civil War
★ 20th Century Wars
★ Civil Rights Movement
★ ESL Lesson - Present Perfect
   Tense

Early Colonists in North America

In 1607 colonists from England arrived on the shores of what is now Virginia and established the settlement of Jamestown. These were mostly aristocratic men looking for **economic opportunities** in the New World. What they found instead were harsh conditions and difficult terrain to plant their crops.

Most of the colonists had either perished or moved to the **Native American** tribes who occupied the lands surrounding the settlement. Between the years 1609-1610 over 80% of the settlers died. This period is called the "starving time."

In 1620 another group of settlers arrived on the shores of the New World looking for something much different: **religious and political freedom**. The Pilgrims, or separatists as they were known, had already fled England and were living in the Netherlands. They decided to sail for America and establish a colony based on their religious beliefs. They are called the Pilgrims.

Before the Pilgrims went ashore, they drafted the Mayflower Compact. This contract promised cooperation among the settlers "for the general good of the Colony unto which we promise all due submission and obedience." Many believe this was the beginning of American democracy. It has been called the world's first written constitution.

Once ashore, the Pilgrims encountered Squanto, a member of the Patuxet tribe. He taught the Pilgrims how to catch eel and grow corn. He also served as an interpreter. In 1621, the Pilgrims and Native Americans celebrated for three days after their first successful harvest. This celebration is considered

U.S. Citizenship and Immigration Services

Civics (History and Government) Questions for the Naturalization Test

1. What is one reason colonists came to America?

2. Who lived in America before the Europeans arrived?

Fun Fact!

Pocohantas was the daughter of one of the Native American chiefs who encountered the settlers in Jamestown.

The Founding Fathers

On **July 4, 1776 Thomas Jefferson** wrote the **Declaration of Independence**. This **declared our independence from Great Britain** and led to the Revolutionary War. The colonists fought the British because **they didn't have self-government**.

The Declaration of Independence was signed by a group of political leaders known as the Founding Fathers. These men were also delegates to the Constitutional Convention in **1787**. The Founding Fathers included Jefferson, George Washington, Benjamin Franklin, James Madison, John Jay, and Alexander Hamilton. **Washington,** called the **"Father of Our Country"**, became the **first president. Madison, Jay, and Hamilton** wrote the **Federalist Papers**, supporting ratification of the Constitution.

Fun Fact!

George Washington was a big man. He was 6 feet 2 inches tall and over 200 pounds.

Benjamin Franklin

Benjamin Franklin was one of the more interesting members of the Founding Fathers. In 1733 he started publishing **"Poor Richard's Almanac."** Almanacs contained weather reports, recipes, predictions, and  homilies. Franklin's almanac was unique because of its lively aphorisms, or sayings. One of his famous sayings was, "A penny saved is a penny earned."

Franklin also helped start the Library Company in 1731. He realized that members could put their money together to buy books from England. This began the nation's **first subscription library.**

After Franklin retired in 1749, he started concentrating on science, in particular electricity. Later in life Franklin served as the **oldest member of the Constitutional Convention** and **U.S. Diplomat.** He died at the age of 84.

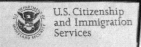
1. What did the Declaration of Independence do?

2. Why did the colonists fight the British?

3. When was the Declaration of Independence adopted?

4. What happened at the Constitutional Convention?

5. When was the Constitution written?

6. Name one of the writers of the Federalist Papers.

7. What is one thing Benjamin Franklin is known for?

Super Stat

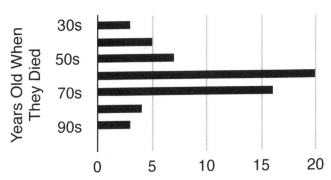

■ How Long The Founding Fathers Lived

Years Old When They Died / Number of Founding Fathers who lived to these ages

The Civil War

Abraham Lincoln was elected president in 1860. At this time many southern states feared that he would abolish the institution of **slavery**. Slavery was vital to the **economy** of the agricultural South. This led to the secession, or withdrawal, of the state of South Carolina in 1861 and the formation of a new government: the Confederate States of America. The Civil War began on April 12, 1861 when the Confederacy refused to surrender Fort Sumter to federal forces. This caused more states to join the Confederacy and the country was divided between the North and South, or free states and slave states.

On January 1, 1863 President Lincoln signed the **Emancipation Proclamation** declaring that all slaves, regardless of where they lived, were free in the eyes of the federal government. In 1865 the Confederacy was losing as Union General Sherman marched through the South destroying everything in his path. On April 9, 1865 Confederate General Robert E. Lee formally surrendered at Appomattox Courthouse and **the war between the states** ended. Five days later President Lincoln was assassinated as he watched a play at Ford's Theater.

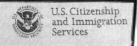

1. Name <u>one</u> war fought by the United States in the 1800s.

2. Name the U.S. war between the North and the South.

3. Name <u>one</u> problem that led to the Civil War.

4. What was <u>one</u> important thing that Abraham Lincoln did?

5. What did the Emancipation Proclamation do?

Super Stat

How People Died During the Civil War

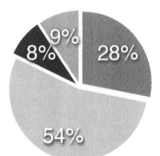

● Killed in Action 28%
○ Died from Disease 54%
● Died as Prisoners 8%
○ Other causes 9%

Twentieth Century Wars

The United States was involved in five wars in **the twentieth century**.

WORLD WAR I

World War I began in 1914 with the assassination of Archduke Franz Ferdinand of Austria. This led to the deaths of millions. The United States, under **President Woodrow Wilson**, joined England, France, and Russia to defeat the Central powers of Germany, Austria-Hungary, and Italy. The outcome of World War I led to the second world war in 1939.

WORLD WAR II

Germany invaded Poland in 1939 and **World War II** began. The United States entered the war on December 7, 1941 when the Japanese navy and air force attacked the U.S. naval base at Pearl Harbor on the territory of Hawaii. **President Franklin Delano Roosevelt** quickly declared war on **Japan, Germany, and Italy**.

Over one hundred countries were involved and nearly ten million Americans participated in the war effort both at home and abroad. **General Dwight D. Eisenhower** and the Allied forces defeated the spread of fascism in Europe and imperialism in Asia in 1945. This led to **the Cold War** to contain the spread of **communism**.

THE KOREAN WAR

The Korean War began on June 25, 1950 when North Korea invaded South Korea across the 38th parallel. The United States and twenty other countries fought alongside the South Korean military until the war ended in 1953.

THE VIETNAM WAR

The United States entered Vietnam in the 1950s to stop the spread of communism. President Lyndon Johnson sent ground troops in 1965 after the Gulf of Tonkin Resolution. However, American troops faced many challenges fighting in the jungle and the United States withdrew its troops in 1973.

PERSIAN GULF WAR

In 1990, Saddam Hussein invaded neighboring Kuwait. This caused the United States and other Western nations to intervene in 1991. After 42 days of air and ground attacks, Iraqi forces fled Kuwait and President George H.W. Bush declared a cease-fire.

Fun Fact!

President during WWII,
Franklin Delano Roosevelt
(FDR) was the only president
to be elected 4 times.

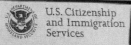

U.S. Citizenship
and Immigration
Services

Civics (History and Government) Questions for the Naturalization Test

1. Name one war fought by the United States in the 1900s.

2. Who was President during World War I?

3. Who was President during the Great Depression and World War II?

4. Who did the United States fight in World War II?

5. Before he was President, Eisenhower was a general. What war was he in?

6. During the Cold War, what was the main concern of the United States?

The Civil Rights Movement

The **civil rights movement** of the 1950s and 1960s aimed to guarantee equality under the law and preserve voter rights for African Americans, especially in the South. A Baptist minister named **Martin Luther King Jr.** was an influential civil rights activist. He promoted non-violent protest and civil disobedience to achieve these goals. He led the 1955 Montgomery Bus Boycott and helped start the Southern Christian Leadership Conference (SCLC) in 1957, serving as its first president.

This led to the Civil Rights Act of 1964 that banned **discrimination** based on "race, color, religion, or national origin" in employment practices and public accommodations. It also led to the Voting Rights Act of 1965 that restored and protected voting rights. On August 28, 1963, King gave his famous "I Have a Dream" speech on the steps of Lincoln Memorial to over 250,000 civil rights supporters. He called for an end to racism in the United States. Martin Luther King, Jr was assassinated on April 4, 1968.

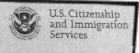
1. **What movement tried to end racial discrimination?**

2. **What did Martin Luther King, Jr. do?**

Excerpt from MLK's "I Have a Dream" Speech

"I have a dream that one day this nation will rise up and live out the true meaning of its creed: "We hold these truths to be self-evident: that all men are created equal." I have a dream that my four children will one day live in a nation where they will not be judged by the color of their skin but by the content of their character. I have a dream today."

The Present Perfect Tense

Use the Present Perfect Tense when talking about events that began in the past and continue into the present time.

ex) I have lived in Los Angeles since 2003.

In this example you started living in Los Angeles in 2003 and you continue to live there in the present.

The Present Perfect is also used in the Progressive or Continuous form:

ex) I have been living in Los Angeles since 2003.

The Present Perfect

Subject	have/has	past participle verb
I, You	have	lived
He, She, It	has	lived
We, They	have	lived

Use black ink.

Here are some examples of the *Present Perfect Tense* taken from the N-400 application.

1. Where <u>have you lived</u> during the last five years?

2. How many times <u>have you been married</u>?

3. How many sons and daughters <u>have you had</u>?

4. <u>Have you ever been</u> in jail or prison?

5. <u>Have you ever served</u> in the U.S. Armed Forces?

Possible Answers to the above Present Perfect Questions.

1. <u>I've lived</u> in New York for the past five years.
2. <u>I've been married</u> only once.
3. <u>I've had</u> two children, one son and one daughter.
4. No, I <u>haven't</u>.
5. No, I <u>haven't</u>.

Your Timeline

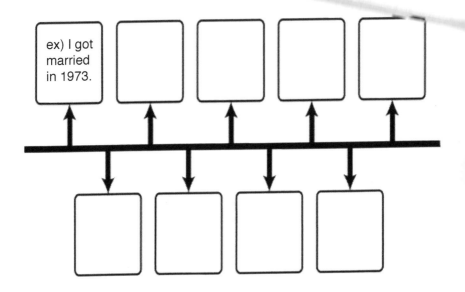

ex) I got married in 1973.

1. **Put nine long term milestones on the TIMELINE above. Then talk about them in the present perfect tense with a partner.**
   ex) *I have been married since 1973.*
   or
   I have worked at my job for ten years.

Verbs

BASE FORM	SIMPLE PAST	PAST PARTICIPLE
be	was/were	been
live	lived	lived
study	studied	studied
work	worked	worked
have	had	had
drive	drove	driven
go	went	gone
take	took	taken
give	gave	given

2. Write 3 sentences about your life using the present perfect.

ex) I have worked at my job for seven years.

1._____

2._____

3._____

3. Complete each sentence in present perfect tense using the verb in parentheses. ( ) Don't forget to use the auxiliary verb *have* or *has*.

1. I _____ at my job for twelve years.
   (work)

2. Joe _____ in the United States since 1995.
   (live)

3. We _____ never _____ to Las Vegas.
   (be)

4. How long _____ Mary _____ piano lessons?
   (take)

5. How long _____ you _____ English?
   (study)

6. My brother and sister _____ that movie yet.
   (not see)

7. _____ you ever _____ to Disneyland?
   (go)

8. _____ John _____ you a birthday present yet?
   (give)

4. Practice the conversation with a partner.

A: Good afternoon. How are you?

B: I'm fine. And you?

A: Fine, thanks. When did you come to the United States?

B: I came to the United States in 2002.

A: And how long have you lived at your current address?

B: My family and I have been there since 2009. We really like it there.

A: Have you ever used another name?

B: No, I haven't.

A: Have you ever failed to file an income tax return?

B: No, I haven't.

A: Ok. That's all. Thank you for coming down today.

Questions and Responses Using Present Perfect
and *ever*

5. Work with a partner to ask and answer the following questions.

Q: Have you *ever* seen the movie Star Wars?

A: Yes, I have. / No, I haven't.

Q: Have you *ever* tried Sushi?

A: Yes, I have. / No, I haven't.

Q: Have you *ever* been to the Grand Canyon?

A: Yes, I have. / No, I haven't.

Q: Have you *ever* found a $100 bill on the street?

A: Yes, I have. / No, I haven't.

Q: Have you *ever* taken a bus?

A: Yes, I have. / No, I haven't.

CHAPTER IV

Civics Extras

★ Writing Vocabulary
★ Reading Vocabulary
★ The Pledge of Allegiance
★ The Star Spangled Banner

WRITING VOCABULARY

For the writing test, you must write one out of three sentences correctly. You may need to use one or more of the following words in your writing.

PEOPLE
Adams   Lincoln   Washington

CIVICS
American Indians   capital   citizens   Civil War
Congress   Father of Our Country   flag   free
freedom of speech   President   right   Senators
state/states   White House

MONTHS
February   May   June
July   September
October   November

VERBS
can   come   elect   have/has
is/was/be
lives/lived   meets   pay
vote   want

OTHER (CONTENT)
blue   dollar bill   fifty/50   first   largest   most
north   one   one hundred/100   people   red
second   south   taxes   white

Writing Vocabulary Continued

PLACES

Alaska   California
Canada   Delaware
Mexico
New York City
United States
Washington
Washington, D.C.

OTHER (FUNCTION)

and during for here
in of on the to we

HOLIDAYS

Presidents' Day
Memorial Day   Flag Day
Independence Day   Labor Day
Columbus Day
Thanksgiving

Unscramble the sentences.

1. in is November. Thanksgiving

_____

2. President. first the was Washington

_____

3. has United States The states. fifty

_____

READING VOCABULARY

For the reading portion, you must read one
out of three sentences correctly. The
sentences you read may contain some of the
following words.

PEOPLE
Abraham Lincoln
George Washington

CIVICS
American flag   Bill of Rights   capital
citizen   city   Congress   country
Father of Our Country   government
President   right   Senators   state/states
White House

PLACES
America
United States
U.S.

HOLIDAYS
President's Day   Memorial Day
Flag Day   Columbus Day
Labor Day   Thanksgiving

QUESTION WORDS
How   What   When
Where   Who   Why

VERBS
can   come   do/does
elects   have/has
is/are/was/be
lives/lived   meet
name   pay   vote
want

Reading Vocabulary Continued

OTHER (FUNCTION)
a for here in of on the to we

OTHER (CONTENT)
colors dollar bill first largest many most north one people second south

Read the sentences.
Which are true?
Which are false?

1. The United States has fifty states.

2. Abraham Lincoln is known as the "Father of Our Country."

3. The President does *not* live in the White House.

4. U.S. citizens 18 and older can vote.

The Pledge of Allegiance

I pledge allegiance to the Flag of the United States of America, and to the republic for which it stands, one Nation **under God,** indivisible, with liberty and justice for all.

The Star-Spangled Banner

The Star-Spangled Banner

Oh, say, can you see, by the dawn's early
light,
What so proudly we hailed at the
twilight's last gleaming?
Whose broad stripes and bright stars,
thro' the perilous fight;
O'er the ramparts we watched, were so
gallantly streaming.
And the rockets red glare, the bombs
bursting in air,
Gave proof through the night that our
flag was still there.
Oh, say, does that star-spangled banner
yet wave
O'er the land of the free and the home
of the brave?

CHAPTER V
Updated Questions/Review

	Application For Naturalization	**USCIS**
	Department of Homeland Security	**Form N-400**
	U.S. Citizenship and Immigration Services	OMB No. 1615-0052
		Expires 09/30/2015

Part 11. Additional Information   A-

Answer Item Numbers 1. - 21. If you answer *"Yes"* to any of these questions, include a written explanation on an additional sheet(s) of paper and provide any evidence to support your answer.

1. Have you **ever** claimed to be a U.S. citizen *(in writing or any other way)*? ☐ Yes ☐ No

2. Have you **ever** registered to vote in any Federal, State, or local election in the United States? ☐ Yes ☐ No

3. Have you **ever** voted in any Federal, State, or local election in the United States? ☐ Yes ☐ No

4. Do you now have, or did you **ever** have, a hereditary title or an order of nobility in any foreign country? ☐ Yes ☐ No

5. Have you **ever** been declared legally incompetent, or been confined to a mental institution? ☐ Yes ☐ No

6. Do you owe any overdue Federal, State, or local taxes? ☐ Yes ☐ No

7. A. Have you **ever** not filed a Federal, State, or local tax return since you became a Permanent Resident? ☐ Yes ☐ No

   B. If *"Yes,"* did you consider yourself to be a "non-U.S. resident"? ☐ Yes ☐ No

8. Have you called yourself a "non-U.S. resident" on a Federal, State, or local tax return since you became a Permanent Resident? ☐ Yes ☐ No

9. A. Have you **ever** been a member of, involved in, or in any way associated with, any organization, association, fund, foundation, party, club, society, or similar group in the United States or in any other ☐ Yes ☐ No

★ Yes/No Questions
★ Reading Review

Beginning in February 2014, the USCIS will use a new 21 page N-400 Application for Naturalization. It includes:

- a section regarding the citizenship status of your parents
- a section to request a waiver to the English Language Requirement
- a section that combines education and work history
- many new questions about terrorism and criminal behavior

Your ability to answer short answer, **yes/no** questions correctly is important for your interview. This section of the textbook will focus on the possible **yes/no** short answer questions that you may be asked during your interview, especially those **yes/no** questions from the N-400, part 11 "Additional Information". The majority of questions in part 11 are questions that begin with **Were you ever, Did you ever,** and **Have you ever.** The more you practice asking and answering these questions, the more comfortable you will be during your interview.

*Remember, this textbook is only intended to assist you with your English language skills and ability to answer questions in English. Citizenship Basics© is NOT intended to give you answers. If you have any doubts about whether to answer a question "yes" or "no", you should consult a professional immigration attorney or counselor.

Use black ink.

Part 11. Additional Information

Here are some examples of yes or no questions in the *Simple Past Tense of the verb "to be"* taken from the N-400 application.

1. Were you ever a worker, volunteer, or soldier in a prison?
2. Were you ever a part of a group that used a weapon against any person?
3. Were you ever a member of a military unit?
4. Were you ever involved in any way with torture?
5. Were you ever involved with not letting someone practice his or her religion?

Possible Answers to the above Simple Present Questions.

1. No, I wasn't.
2. No, I wasn't.
3. No, I wasn't.
4. No, I wasn't.
5. No, I wasn't.

1. Work with a partner to ask and answer the following *"were you ever…"* questions.

Q: Were you *ever* denied a credit card?

A: Yes, I was./No, I wasn't.

> **ever** = at any time

Q: Were you *ever* late for work?

A: Yes, I was./No, I wasn't.

Q: Were you *ever* proud of something you accomplished?

A: Yes, I was./No, I wasn't.

Q: Were you *ever* in love with someone who didn't love you?

A: Yes, I was./No, I wasn't.

Q: Were you *ever* afraid to tell someone the truth?

A: Yes, I was./No, I wasn't.

Q: Were you *ever* on TV?

A: Yes, I was./No, I wasn't.

Q: Were you *ever* in the hospital?

A: Yes, I was./No, I wasn't.

N-400 Application for Naturalization

Use black ink.

Part 11. Additional Information

Here are some examples of yes or no questions in the *Simple Past Tense* (<u>not</u> the verb "to be") taken from the N-400 application.

1. Did you ever sell weapons to any person?
2. Did you ever receive any type of military training?
3. Did you ever ask any person under the age of fifteen to serve in an armed group?
4. Did you ever help another person provide weapons to any person?
5. Did you ever work for the Nazi government of Germany?

Possible Answers to the above Simple Past Questions.

1. No, I <u>didn't</u>.
2. No, I <u>didn't</u>.
3. No, I <u>didn't</u>.
4. No, I <u>didn't</u>.
5. No, I <u>didn't</u>.

1. Work with a partner to ask and answer the following *"Did you ever..."* questions.

Q: Did you *ever* forget someone's name?

A: Yes, I did./No, I didn't.

ever = at any time

Q: Did you *ever* forget to pay a bill?

A: Yes, I did./No, I didn't.

Q: Did you *ever* read *The Hunger Games*?

A: Yes, I did./No, I didn't.

Q: Did you *ever* find a wallet on the street?

A: Yes, I did./No, I didn't.

Q: Did you *ever* get a compliment for a new haircut?

A: Yes, I did./No, I didn't.

Q: Did you *ever* feel like you didn't belong in a place?

A: Yes, I did./No, I didn't.

Q: Did you *ever* stop to smell the roses?

A: Yes, I did./No, I didn't.

N-400 Application for Naturalization

Use black ink.

Part 11. Additional Information

Here are some examples of yes/no questions in the *Present Perfect* taken from the N-400 application.

1. Have you ever persecuted any person because of religion?
2. Have you ever been arrested?
3. Have you ever been convicted of a crime?
4. Have you ever been placed in a rehabilitative program?
5. Have you ever been placed on probation?

Possible Answers to the above Simple Past Questions.

1. No, I haven't.
2. No, I haven't.
3. No, I haven't.
4. No, I haven't.
5. No, I haven't.

1. Work with a partner to ask and answer the following *"have you ever..."* questions.

Q: Have you *ever* run a marathon?

> **ever** = at any time

A: Yes, I have./No, I haven't.

Q: Have you *ever* played golf?

A: Yes, I have./No, I haven't.

Q: Have you *ever* rented a car?

A: Yes, I have./No, I haven't.

Q: Have you *ever* been to the circus?

A: Yes, I have./No, I haven't.

Q: Have you *ever* been bullied?

A: Yes, I have./No, I haven't.

Q: Have you *ever* driven a truck?

A: Yes, I have./No, I haven't.

Q: Have you *ever* milked a cow?

A: Yes, I have./No, I haven't.

2. Work alone or with a partner to answer the following *"were you ever," "did you ever,"* and *"have you ever"* questions. Answer the 'yes/no' questions using the correct form of the past tense or present perfect tense as fast as you can.

Q: **Did** you *ever* open someone's mail on accident?

Q: **Were** you *ever* in Hawaii?

Q: **Did** you *ever* open a strange email?

Q: **Have** you *ever* tried Thai food?

Q: **Were** you *ever* at an office Christmas party?

Q: **Were** you *ever* so nervous that you couldn't speak?

Q: **Did** you *ever* text a picture of yourself to someone?

Q: **Have** you *ever* purchased anything on Ebay?

Q: **Were** you *ever* at the beach when it rained?

Q: **Did** you *ever* take an algebra class?

Q: **Did** you *ever* go to church when you were younger?

Q: **Have** you *ever* flown in a helicopter?

Q: **Were** you *ever* a chef in a restaurant?

Q: **Did** you *ever* see a funny cat video?

3. Work alone or with a partner to answer the following *yes/no*, short answer questions that utilize all verbs tenses covered in this book.

Q: Are you married?

Q: Is this your last name?

Q: Do you have a photo ID?

Q: Are you requesting any accommodations?

Q: Are you 50 years of age or older?

Q: Is this your correct address?

Q: Are your parents U.S. Citizens?

Q: Does your spouse still live at this address?

Q: Are your eyes brown?

Q: Have you ever voted in a Federal election in the United States?

Q: Do you owe any taxes?

Q: Were you ever involved in genocide?

Q: Did you ever work for the Nazi government of Germany?

Q: Did you ever receive any military training?

Q: Have you ever been convicted of an offense?

Q: Are deportation proceedings currently pending against you?

Q: Have you ever gambled illegally?

Q: Do you support the Constitution?

Q: Are you willing to take the full Oath of Allegiance to the United States?

Q: Do you understand the full Oath of Allegiance to the United States?

Reading Review

3. Refer to the readings from the previous chapters to fill in the missing words.

1. The Constitution was drafted in _____ and begins with the words "We the_____."

2. The first ten _____ to the Constitution are called the _____ of Rights and guarantee certain rights to all people living in the United States.

3. The President is in charge of the _____ Branch of the United States government and is elected every _____ years in _____.

4. The _____ Amendment guaranteed the right to _____ regardless of race, color, or previous condition of servitude.

5. President Franklin Delano _____ quickly declared war on Japan, Germany, and _____.

6. On July 4, 17____ Thomas _____ wrote the Declaration of Independence.

7. On January 1, 1863 President _____ signed the Emancipation _____ declaring that all_____, regardless of where they lived, were _____ in the eyes of the federal government.

Answers to ESL Lessons

Page 17
1. work
2. lives
3. live
4. have
5. drive
6. study
7. go
8. takes

Page 30
1. worked
2. lived
3. live
4. have
5. drove
6. study
7. go
8. took

Page 50
1. have worked
2. has lived
3. have...been
4. has...taken
5. have...studied
6. haven't seen
7. Have...gone
8. Has...given

Page 55
1. Thanksgiving is in November.
2. Washington was the first President.
3. The United States has fifty states.

Page 57
1. T
2. F
3. F
4. T

Page 71
1. 1787, People
2. amendments, Bill,
3. Executive, four, November
4. 15th, vote,
5. Roosevelt, Italy
6. 76, Jefferson
7. Lincoln, Proclamation, slaves, free

100 Questions

Civics (History and Government) Questions for the
Naturalization Test
The 100 civics (history and government) questions and
answers for the naturalization test are listed below.

AMERICAN GOVERNMENT
A: Principles of American Democracy

1. What is the supreme law of the land?
- the Constitution

2. What does the Constitution do?
- sets up the government
- defines the government
- protects basic rights of Americans

*3. The idea of self-government is in the first three
words of the Constitution. What are these words?*
- We the People

4. What is an amendment?
- a change (to the Constitution)
- an addition (to the Constitution)

*5. What do we call the first ten amendments to the
Constitution?*
- the Bill of Rights

*6. What is one right or freedom from the First
Amendment?**
- speech
- religion
- assembly
- press
- petition the government

7. How many amendments does the Constitution have?
- twenty-seven (27)

8. What did the Declaration of Independence do?
- announced our independence (from Great Britain)
- declared our independence (from Great Britain)
- said that the United States is free (from Great Britain)

9. What are two rights in the Declaration of Independence?
- life
- liberty
- pursuit of happiness

10. What is freedom of religion?
- You can practice any religion, or not practice a religion.

11. What is the economic system in the United States?*
- capitalist economy
- market economy

12. What is the "rule of law"?
- Everyone must follow the law.
- Leaders must obey the law.
- Government must obey the law.
- No one is above the law.

B: System of Government

13. *Name one branch or part of the government.* *
- Congress
- legislative
- President
- executive
- the courts
- judicial

14. *What stops one branch of government from becoming too powerful?*
- checks and balances
- separation of powers

15. *Who is in charge of the executive branch?*
- the President

16. *Who makes federal laws?*
- Congress
- Senate and House (of Representatives)
- (U.S. or national) legislature

17. *What are the two parts of the U.S. Congress?* *
- the Senate and House (of Representatives)

18. *How many U.S. Senators are there?*
- one hundred (100)

19. *We elect a U.S. Senator for how many years?*
- six (6)

20. Who is one of your state's U.S. Senators now?*
- Answers will vary. [District of Columbia residents and residents of U.S. Territories should answer that D.C. (or the territory where the applicant lives) has no U.S. Senators.]

21. The House of Representatives has how many voting members?
- four hundred thirty-five (435)

22. We elect a U.S. Representative for how many years?
- two (2)

23. Name your U.S. Representative.
- Answers will vary. [Residents of territories with nonvoting Delegates or Resident Commissioners may provide the name of that Delegate or Commissioner. Also acceptable is any statement that the territory has no (voting) Representatives in Congress.]

24. Who does a U.S. Senator represent?
- all people of the state

25. Why do some states have more Representatives than other states?
- (because of) the state's population
- (because) they have more people
- (because) some states have more people

26. We elect a President for how many years?
- four (4)

27. In what month do we vote for President?*
- November

28. What is the name of the President of the United States now?*
- Barack Obama
- Obama

29. What is the name of the Vice President of the United States now?
- Joseph R. Biden, Jr.
- Joe Biden
- Biden

30. If the President can no longer serve, who becomes President?
- the Vice President

31. If both the President and the Vice President can no longer serve, who becomes President?
- the Speaker of the House

32. Who is the Commander in Chief of the military?
- the President

33. Who signs bills to become laws?
- the President

34. Who vetoes bills?
- the President

35. What does the President's Cabinet do?
- advises the President

36. What are two Cabinet-level positions?
- Secretary of Agriculture
- Secretary of Commerce
- Secretary of Defense
- Secretary of Education
- Secretary of Energy
- Secretary of Health and Human Services
- Secretary of Homeland Security
- Secretary of Housing and Urban Development
- Secretary of the Interior
- Secretary of Labor
- Secretary of State
- Secretary of Transportation
- Secretary of the Treasury
- Secretary of Veterans Affairs
- Attorney General
- Vice President

37. What does the judicial branch do?
- reviews laws
- explains laws
- resolves disputes (disagreements)
- decides if a law goes against the Constitution

38. What is the highest court in the United States?
- the Supreme Court

39. How many justices are on the Supreme Court?
- nine (9)

40. Who is the Chief Justice of the United States now?
- John Roberts (John G. Roberts, Jr.)

41. *Under our Constitution, some powers belong to the federal government. What is one power of the federal government?*
- to print money
- to declare war
- to create an army
- to make treaties

42. *Under our Constitution, some powers belong to the states. What is one power of the states?*
- provide schooling and education
- provide protection (police)
- provide safety (fire departments)
- give a driver's license
- approve zoning and land use

43. *Who is the Governor of your state now?*
- Answers will vary. [District of Columbia residents should answer that D.C. does not have a Governor.]

44. *What is the capital of your state?**
- Answers will vary. [District of Columbia residents should answer that D.C. is not a state and does not have a capital. Residents of U.S. territories should name the capital of the territory.]

45. *What are the two major political parties in the United States?**
- Democratic and Republican

46. *What is the political party of the President now?*
- Democratic (Party)

47. What is the name of the Speaker of the House of Representatives now?
- (John) Boehner

C: Rights and Responsibilities

48. There are four amendments to the Constitution about who can vote. Describe one of them.
- Citizens eighteen (18) and older (can vote).
- You don't have to pay (a poll tax) to vote.
- Any citizen can vote. (Women and men can vote.)
- A male citizen of any race (can vote).

49. What is one responsibility that is only for United States citizens?*
- serve on a jury
- vote in a federal election

50. Name one right only for United States citizens.
- vote in a federal election
- run for federal office

51. What are two rights of everyone living in the United States?
- freedom of expression
- freedom of speech
- freedom of assembly
- freedom to petition the government
- freedom of worship
- the right to bear arms

52. *What do we show loyalty to when we say the Pledge of Allegiance?*
- the United States
- the flag

53. *What is one promise you make when you become a United States citizen?*
- give up loyalty to other countries
- defend the Constitution and laws of the United States
- obey the laws of the United States
- serve in the U.S. military (if needed)
- serve (do important work for) the nation (if needed)
- be loyal to the United States

54. *How old do citizens have to be to vote for President?**
- eighteen (18) and older

55. *What are two ways that Americans can participate in their democracy?*
- vote
- join a political party
- help with a campaign
- join a civic group
- join a community group
- give an elected official your opinion on an issue
- call Senators and Representatives
- publicly support or oppose an issue or policy
- run for office
- write to a newspaper

56. *When is the last day you can send in federal income tax forms?**
- April 15

57. *When must all men register for the Selective Service?*
- at age eighteen (18)
- between eighteen (18) and twenty-six (26)

AMERICAN HISTORY
A: Colonial Period and Independence

58. *What is one reason colonists came to America?*
- freedom
- political liberty
- religious freedom
- economic opportunity
- practice their religion
- escape persecution

59. *Who lived in America before the Europeans arrived?*
- American Indians
- Native Americans

60. *What group of people was taken to America and sold as slaves?*
- Africans
- people from Africa

61. Why did the colonists fight the British?
- because of high taxes (taxation without representation)
- because the British army stayed in their houses (boarding, quartering)
- because they didn't have self-government

62. Who wrote the Declaration of Independence?
- (Thomas) Jefferson

63. When was the Declaration of Independence adopted?
- July 4, 1776

64. There were 13 original states. Name three.
- New Hampshire
- Massachusetts
- Rhode Island
- Connecticut
- New York
- New Jersey
- Pennsylvania
- Delaware
- Maryland
- Virginia
- North Carolina
- South Carolina
- Georgia

65. What happened at the Constitutional Convention?
- The Constitution was written.
- The Founding Fathers wrote the Constitution.

66. *When was the Constitution written?*
- 1787

67. *The Federalist Papers supported the passage of the U.S. Constitution. Name one of the writers.*
- (James) Madison
- (Alexander) Hamilton
- (John) Jay
- Publius

68. *What is one thing Benjamin Franklin is famous for?*
- U.S. diplomat
- oldest member of the Constitutional Convention
- first Postmaster General of the United States
- writer of "Poor Richard's Almanac"
- started the first free libraries

69. *Who is the "Father of Our Country"?*
- (George) Washington

70. *Who was the first President?**
- (George) Washington

B: 1800s

71. *What territory did the United States buy from France in 1803?*
- the Louisiana Territory
- Louisiana

72. *Name one war fought by the United States in the 1800s.*
- War of 1812
- Mexican-American War
- Civil War
- Spanish-American War

73. *Name the U.S. war between the North and the South.*
- the Civil War
- the War between the States

74. *Name one problem that led to the Civil War.*
- slavery
- economic reasons
- states' rights

75. *What was one important thing that Abraham Lincoln did?**
- freed the slaves (Emancipation Proclamation)
- saved (or preserved) the Union
- led the United States during the Civil War

76. *What did the Emancipation Proclamation do?*
- freed the slaves
- freed slaves in the Confederacy
- freed slaves in the Confederate states
- freed slaves in most Southern states

77. *What did Susan B. Anthony do?*
- fought for women's rights
- fought for civil rights

78. Name one war fought by the United States in the 1900s.*

- World War I
- World War II
- Korean War
- Vietnam War
- (Persian) Gulf War

79. Who was President during World War I?

- (Woodrow) Wilson

80. Who was President during the Great Depression and World War II?

- (Franklin) Roosevelt

81. Who did the United States fight in World War II?

- Japan, Germany, and Italy

82. Before he was President, Eisenhower was a general. What war was he in?

- World War II

83. During the Cold War, what was the main concern of the United States?

- Communism

84. What movement tried to end racial discrimination?

- civil rights (movement)

85. What did Martin Luther King, Jr. do?*

- fought for civil rights
- worked for equality for all Americans

86. What major event happened on September 11, 2001, in the United States?
- Terrorists attacked the United States.

87. Name one American Indian tribe in the United States.
[USCIS Officers will be supplied with a list of federally recognized American Indian tribes.]
- Cherokee
- Navajo
- Sioux
- Chippewa
- Choctaw
- Pueblo
- Apache
- Iroquois
- Creek
- Blackfeet
- Seminole
- Cheyenne
- Arawak
- Shawnee
- Mohegan
- Huron
- Oneida
- Lakota
- Crow
- Teton
- Hopi
- Inuit

INTEGRATED CIVICS
A. Geography

88. *Name one of the two longest rivers in the United States.*
- Missouri (River)
- Mississippi (River)

89. *What ocean is on the West Coast of the United States?*
- Pacific (Ocean)

90. *What ocean is on the East Coast of the United States?*
- Atlantic (Ocean)

91. *Name one U.S. territory.*
- Puerto Rico
- U.S. Virgin Islands
- American Samoa
- Northern Mariana Islands
- Guam

92. *Name one state that borders Canada.*
- Maine
- New Hampshire
- Vermont
- New York
- Pennsylvania
- Ohio
- Michigan
- Minnesota
- North Dakota
- Montana

- Idaho
- Washington
- Alaska

93. Name one state that borders Mexico.
- California
- Arizona
- New Mexico
- Texas

94. What is the capital of the United States?*
- Washington, D.C.

95. Where is the Statue of Liberty?*
- New York (Harbor)
- Liberty Island

[Also acceptable are New Jersey, near New York City, and on the Hudson (River).]

B: Symbols

96. Why does the flag have 13 stripes?
- because there were 13 original colonies
- because the stripes represent the original colonies

97. Why does the flag have 50 stars?*
- because there is one star for each state
- because each star represents a state
- because there are 50 states

98. What is the name of the national anthem?
- The Star-Spangled Banner

C: Holidays

*99. When do we celebrate Independence Day?**
- July 4

100. Name two national U.S. holidays.
- New Year's Day
- Martin Luther King, Jr. Day
- Presidents' Day
- Memorial Day
- Independence Day
- Labor Day
- Columbus Day
- Veterans Day
- Thanksgiving
- Christmas

* If you are 65 years old or older and have been a legal permanent resident of the United States for 20 or more years, you
may study just the questions that have been marked with an asterisk.